MIRACLES OF MY LIFE

ELIZABETH MARIETTA SAMUH

Copyright © *Elizabeth Marietta Samuh,* 2025

All Rights Reserved

This book is subject to the condition that no part of this book is to be reproduced, transmitted in any form or means; electronic or mechanical, stored in a retrieval system, photocopied, recorded, scanned, or otherwise. Any of these actions require the proper written permission of the author.

TABLE OF CONTENTS

Introduction 1

Chapter 1 A Fractured Beginning 3

Chapter 2 Misunderstood and Labelled 7

Chapter 3 Family and Community 12

Chapter 4 Mothrhood 16

Chapter 5 Education 22

Chapter 6 Spirituality 27

Chapter 7 Overcoming Barriers 31

Chapter 8 Embracing Success 36

Chapter 9: A New Chapter: Living with Purpose 45

Chapter 10: Epilogue 49

Introduction

This book is a true story about living with mental illness. It is a story of strength, hope, and the amazing ability of the human spirit to keep going, even in hard times.

The author has been diagnosed with schizophrenia, a serious mental illness that affects thoughts, feelings, and behaviour. She shares her personal journey—the struggles she has faced, the times she felt misunderstood, and the hurt of being judged unfairly. She also shares the victories she has achieved, such as raising children, going to school, and finding love.

Life has not been easy for her. She has faced many difficult moments, times when she felt lost, alone, and afraid. But she never gave up. She kept moving forward, holding on to hope, and believing that things could get better. Her story is one of courage and determination.

This book is for anyone who has been affected by mental illness—whether personally or through a loved one. It is also for those who work with people who struggle with mental health challenges. By reading this book, you will gain a deeper understanding of what it means to live with mental illness. You will see the pain, but also the strength. You will see the hardships, but also the victories.

Most of all, this book is about hope. No matter how dark things may seem, there is always a way forward. The author's journey proves that, with courage and support, it is possible to live a meaningful and fulfilling life.

– Elizabeth Samuh

Chapter 1
A Fractured Beginning

My story begins in the bustling city of London, where I was born. However, my time with my biological family was short-lived. At just three months old, I was fostered by a white family in Berkshire. While the reasons behind this separation remain unclear, the distance that grew between me and my biological family would shape the course of my life in profound ways.

Eventually, my biological parents regained custody of me, and I was brought back into a family that felt more like a collection of strangers than a source of warmth and belonging. I had three sisters, but we were never close. It always felt like there was a wall between us. They had their bond, their shared moments, but I was always on the outside looking in. My parents' relationship was stormy—filled with arguments, tension, and sometimes even danger. The constant fighting and negativity in our home weighed heavily on me, and I felt its impact deeply. It shaped how I saw the world, how I saw myself.

The relationships in my biological family were full of ups and downs, with constant arguments and tension between my parents. There were times when the house felt like a battleground, filled with shouting, anger, and uneasy silence. Their fights created a stressful and unsettling environment, making it hard for me to feel safe or at peace. I never knew what to expect—one moment, things might seem calm, and the next, everything would erupt into chaos.

Seeing these intense arguments made me feel constantly on edge, never knowing what would happen next. Instead of feeling safe and secure like a child should, I felt like my world was unstable, always shifting beneath me. I longed for a peaceful home, a place where I could relax without fear, but that sense of comfort always seemed far away. No matter how much I wished for things to be different, the chaos never stopped, leaving me feeling lost and unsure of where I truly belonged.

On top of everything else, my sisters made me the target of their bullying. They would laugh at me in a way that felt sharp and painful, breaking my heart a little more each time. My self-esteem, already weak, crumbled even further. I never understood why they treated me this way, and the confusion only made it hurt more. No matter how hard I tried to fit in or please them, nothing changed. Their cruel words and actions pushed me deeper into loneliness, making me feel smaller and more invisible every day. With each insult, each laugh at my expense, I withdrew further into myself, losing the little confidence I had left.

School was no escape from the loneliness and pain I felt at home. Instead of finding comfort, I faced the same cruelty from my classmates. It was as if they could sense my weakness, just like my sisters did, and they took every chance to mock and intimidate me. I never understood why they treated me this way—I had done nothing to deserve it. All I wanted was a friend, someone who would listen and understand, but no one ever came. Surrounded by so many people, I still felt completely alone, drowning in a world that seemed cold and unwelcoming.

Coming home every day didn't make things any better. Instead of feeling safe or welcomed, I felt like a stranger in my own family. My parents and sisters were close, moving together as if they belonged to a world I wasn't a part of. No matter how much I wanted to be included, there was always a distance between us. When I tried to talk about my feelings—about how lonely and hurt I was—no one seemed to care. My words felt invisible, as if they didn't matter, as if I didn't matter. No matter how hard I tried to be seen and heard, it was as if I wasn't really there at all.

The pain of everything I was going through started to show in ways I couldn't control. Even the simplest tasks, like washing myself, felt impossible. I no longer had the energy or will to take care of myself. A deep hatred for who I was began to grow inside me, filling my mind with cruel thoughts. I started to believe that I was worthless, that I didn't belong anywhere. The sadness became so heavy that I began to wonder if the only way to escape it was to disappear completely. Dark thoughts of ending my own life crept in, a frightening sign of just how lost and hopeless I felt.

This was my life—a childhood filled with loneliness, neglect, and emotional pain. I felt like I had no one to turn to, no place where I truly belonged. Each day was a struggle, weighed down by sadness and a constant feeling of being unwanted. In this harsh and empty world, the early signs of mental illness began to grow, taking hold in my heart and mind. My wounded spirit became the perfect place for these struggles to take root, shaping the way I saw myself and the world around me.

Chapter 2
Misunderstood and Labelled

From a young age, I carried the weight of being misunderstood—a heavy burden made of fear and judgment. When I was just seven, something happened to me—an assault that, in my innocence, I couldn't fully understand. I didn't know what it meant at the time, but it left a mark on me, shaping my fears and insecurities in ways I wouldn't realize until much later.

School should have been a place where I could learn and grow, but instead, it felt like a battlefield—one I created in my own mind. I constantly felt misunderstood, convinced that others saw me as "stupid." That word, though no one had actually called me that, echoed in my thoughts like a cruel taunt. The fear of proving it true made me second-guess everything I did. I became clumsy, hesitant, always afraid that every mistake confirmed what I dreaded most—that I wasn't good enough.

Even moments that should have felt safe—like studying with my dad and sisters—were clouded by fear. Instead of comfort, I felt pressure, as if every mistake proved I wasn't good enough. I was constantly afraid of failing, of disappointing the people I loved, of messing up in a way I couldn't fix. It felt like my own mind had turned against me, filling my head with doubts I couldn't escape.

At home, the feeling of being misunderstood only grew stronger. I was seen—maybe not intentionally, but often enough—as "no good to the family." Whether those words were said in frustration or simply implied, they sank deep into my heart. I started to believe them. Over time, they shaped the way I saw myself, the way I acted, and the way I interacted with others. It was as if I was living out a story that had already been written for me—one where I was never enough.

In my twenties, the cycle of misunderstanding didn't stop. The way I spoke or expressed myself—things that came from a place of innocence—were often taken the wrong way. It felt like people saw something in me that wasn't there, as if I deserved to be treated harshly, like a bully in disguise. No matter what I did, I couldn't shake the feeling that I was being judged unfairly. It made forming real connections difficult and chipped away at what little self-esteem I had left.

My first experience with love ended in heartbreak—and even more entanglement with social services. I fell in love, got pregnant, and was quickly met with the harsh reality of my situation. With no job and labelled as unfit to be a parent, I was told that terminating the pregnancy was my best option. The weight of that suggestion, the bleakness of my circumstances, and the complete lack of support made me feel more alone than ever. It was overwhelming, like I was being backed into a corner with no way out.

Desperate for connection and stability, I turned to a dating agency, hoping to find something real—something safe. But instead, it led to another disaster. I became pregnant again, and the emotional chaos that followed pushed me to the breaking point. I was admitted to a psychiatric hospital, where heavy medication blurred the world around me, making everything feel both unreal and terrifying.

Through the haze, one thing remained clear—my baby was still growing inside me, surviving despite everything. But when the pregnancy ended, so did my hope. The father, the man I had met through the agency, took the child and cut me out completely. Just like that, my baby was gone. The pain was indescribable, a loss so deep it left me hollow. I was left with nothing but an aching emptiness that I didn't know how to fill.

Through all the chaos, one thing never left me—the label of "mad woman." It followed me like a shadow, whispered behind cupped hands, lingering in the judgmental glances of those who never took the time to understand. No matter how much I tried to prove otherwise, it clung to me.

Still searching for security, for something to hold onto, I became pregnant again. But like before, the child was taken, placed for adoption. Even as I made progress in the psychiatric hospital—finding moments of clarity through medication and therapy—it didn't seem to matter. The system had already decided: I wasn't fit to be a mother. And no matter how much I improved, the stigma never faded.

Within the walls of the psychiatric hospital, I finally found a small sense of understanding—or at least, more than I had felt anywhere else. The medication helped quiet the storm inside me, and therapy gave me a space to untangle the roots of my pain and confusion. For the first time, I felt like I was starting to make sense of my own story.

But even here, misunderstanding found me again. A misdiagnosis of paranoid schizophrenia became yet another label, another weight I had to carry. Though meant to help, it only added to the feeling that I was being seen through a distorted lens. The staff treated me differently, their perception of me shaped by this diagnosis rather than by who I really was. It reinforced the isolation, the fear that no matter how much I improved, I would always be defined by my struggles—trapped in a version of myself that wasn't fully me.

The misdiagnosis affected me deeply, adding yet another layer of struggle to an already overwhelming situation. Even though it wasn't accurate, the label carried weight—far more than I could have imagined. The stigma surrounding schizophrenia was immense, and once it was attached to me, it shaped everything: how others saw me, how I saw myself, and how I tried to move forward.

It wasn't just a word on a medical file—it became a barrier between me and the world. Relationships felt even harder to maintain, and the idea of building a life outside the hospital seemed more impossible than ever. I wasn't just trapped by the system—I was trapped by the label itself, by the way it made me doubt my own reality, my own worth, and my ability to ever be free.

The pain of losing my daughter, my first child, never left me. It was an ache that lived in my heart, a wound that never truly healed. Knowing that I would never get to be her mother, that I had been deemed unfit, was a weight I carried every day. It wasn't just the loss of a child—it was the loss of the life I had hoped for, the proof, in my mind, that I had failed.

The system, though perhaps well-intentioned, had taken my children from me. And in doing so, it had taken a piece of me, leaving behind an emptiness I couldn't fill. My twenties felt like a slow descent into darkness—one misunderstanding after another, one loss piling onto the next. The labels, the misdiagnoses, the constant feeling of being judged and dismissed—it all shaped me, leaving me broken and unbearably alone. The pain wasn't just emotional; it was woven into my very existence, a reminder of everything I had lost.

Chapter 3
Family and Community

Holidays are often painted as times of joy, unity, and cherished memories, but for me, Christmas and Easter carried a different weight. Whenever I gathered with my sisters and Mum during these seasons, an undercurrent of unease shadowed the festivities. Even in my forties, I found myself treated not as an equal, but as a child—infantilised, scapegoated, and perpetually on the outside of the family circle. These experiences left deep marks, eroding my confidence and self-esteem, leading to self-neglect, and fostering a lingering sense of injustice and misunderstanding that has followed me far beyond those holiday moments. The holiday season always began with a flicker of hope that perhaps this time would be different. But as the familiar rituals unfolded, so did the same unsettling patterns. The house would buzz with the warmth of a crackling fire and the aroma of festive meals, yet I couldn't shake a slight paranoia that gnawed at me. My sisters, poised and accomplished, would swap stories of their lives while my mum listened with rapt attention. I sat there, forty-plus years old, waiting for an opening to belong.

One Easter holiday, we were gathered around the table, the clink of cutlery was in the air. I mustered the courage to share something about my life, an achievement I had made at work. Before I could finish, my mum interjected with a gentle but dismissive, "Oh, that's sweet," her tone dripping with the kind of indulgence you'd offer a toddler showing off a finger painting. My sisters barely glanced my way, their conversation swiftly moving on as if I hadn't spoken. The moment stung, and it is when I realised that my voice didn't carry the same weight. Later, as we exchanged gifts, I handed my sister something I'd picked out with care, hoping it might spark a connection. She unwrapped it, offered a perfunctory "thanks," and then turned to admire something else, leaving my effort unnoticed. It wasn't just about the gift; it was the pattern—my presence reduced to an afterthought, my place in the family perpetually questioned. I wasn't a peer or a valued member; I was the baby, the one who didn't quite fit, no matter how many years passed.

This treatment wasn't random—it felt deliberate, intentional. I was the scapegoat, the one blamed when things went awry, the easy target for subtle jabs or outright exclusion. If a holiday plan fell apart or tensions simmered, somehow it circled back to me—an unspoken agreement that I was the misfit. My attempts to contribute or assert myself were met with eye rolls or patronising smiles, as if my age and experiences counted for nothing. I tried to bridge the gap. I'd arrive with stories prepared, questions to ask, anything to prove I belonged. But the responses were always the same—faint amusement or outright indifference. The paranoia I felt wasn't baseless; it was born from years of being treated differently, of watching my sisters be celebrated while I was quietly pushed aside. The message was clear:

I was never to be accepted as part of the family, not in the way I longed to be.

That realisation settled like a stone in my chest. If my own family couldn't see me as an equal, what did that say about me? The belief took root, and with it came a lack of self-esteem that shadowed my every step. Self-neglect followed naturally. I stopped investing in myself—why bother when I didn't feel worthy? Opportunities slipped by, like a job promotion I didn't pursue because I couldn't silence the voice whispering I'd fail. My needs—emotional, physical, even basic care—fell by the wayside, neglected as I internalized the idea that I didn't deserve better. The holidays had taught me a lesson I couldn't unlearn: I was less than, and that belief became a lens through which I viewed everything.

The effects didn't stop at my front door. The sense of being misunderstood and the sting of injustice spilled over into my life beyond the family. I began to see the world as a place where acceptance was for others, not me. Friendships felt fragile, as if I was waiting for people to uncover the flaws my family had already deemed undeniable. At work, I shrank from recognition, convinced I'd be exposed as inadequate. The community around me, which could have been a refuge, instead felt like an extension of the same judgment I'd faced at home. I suffered in silence, carrying the weight of being perpetually misunderstood. The unfairness of it all gnawed at me—why was I the one sidelined, blamed, dismissed? The holidays had planted a seed of doubt that grew into a broader conviction: belonging was something I'd never fully grasp, whether within my family or outside it.

Looking back, I see how those Christmas and Easter gatherings shaped me—for better or worse. The paranoia I felt wasn't imagined; it was a response to years of being cast as the outsider in my own family. At forty-plus, I should have been secure in who I was, yet their treatment kept me tethered to a version of myself I'd outgrown but couldn't shed. The lack of confidence, the self-neglect, the suffering from injustice—these are the legacies of those holidays, burdens I've carried long after the last guest left. But in naming them, in tracing their roots back to those moments, I begin to see them for what they are: not reflections of my worth, but echoes of a dynamic I didn't create. My family's inability to accept me doesn't define me—it reveals their limits, not mine. The journey forward isn't clear, and the pain of exclusion lingers. Yet, there's a quiet strength in recognizing this truth. I may never find the acceptance I sought at that holiday table, but perhaps I can forge it elsewhere—within myself, and in the spaces I choose to call my own. For now, that's enough to hold onto, a flicker of possibility amid the shadows of the past.

Chapter 4
Mothrhood

The anticipation of becoming a mother was a radiant, all-consuming joy, a golden thread woven through every moment of my pregnancy. For nine months, I carried my daughter within me, marveling at her tiny kicks and flutters, each one a whispered promise of the life we would share. I dreamed of her arrival incessantly—her first cry piercing the stillness, her first smile lighting up my world, the way her delicate fingers would curl around mine in trust. I envisioned us nestled in a baby unit, surrounded by the soft glow of pastel blankets and the soothing hum of lullabies, a sacred space where I could learn the tender art of motherhood. The world, I thought, should pause to celebrate this miracle, this perfect being who had already claimed my heart.

But instead of celebration, I was thrust into a nightmare so surreal it felt like a betrayal of everything I held dear. The moment my daughter entered the world, the joy I had nurtured for months was shattered by cold, accusing stares. Whispers morphed into shouts, and before I could cradle her close, before I could whisper a single lullaby into her tiny ear, I was branded a threat. They claimed I would harm her—my own child—that I would beat her, that I was unfit to be her mother. The allegations were sharp as knives, slicing through the core of my identity, leaving wounds no bandage could heal. I stood in that sterile hospital room, the harsh fluorescent lights buzzing overhead, my arms aching to hold her, my voice trembling as I tried to protest. How could anyone believe such lies? I loved her with a ferocity that consumed me, a love so pure it defied comprehension. Yet, there I was, powerless, watching as the system that should have safeguarded us turned its back on me.

The accusations weren't just personal—they were a reflection of a deeper societal flaw. Mothers are held to impossible standards, expected to embody perfection, to suppress any hint of vulnerability. When we stumble, when the weight of postpartum emotions presses down, we're not met with compassion but with judgment. My story is one of many, a chorus of silenced voices—women whose struggles are dismissed, whose humanity is overlooked. The system didn't seek to understand me; it had already decided my fate, and I was swept away in its merciless current.

That current carried me to a psychiatric hospital, a place promised as a sanctuary of healing but revealed as a prison of despair. The corridors were stark and sterile, reeking of antiseptic, their gray walls closing in like a vice. The staff moved with detached efficiency, their faces blank, their voices clipped, as if my presence was a inconvenience they'd rather erase. The other patients eyed me with suspicion, their gazes heavy with unspoken accusations, as though I carried some contagious flaw. I was an outsider, trapped in a world that despised me. Each day bled into the next, a monotonous cycle of forced medication and hollow routine. They handed me pills without explanation, bitter tablets that coated my tongue and dulled my mind. I didn't want them, didn't need them, but consent was a luxury I wasn't afforded. The drugs clouded my senses, turning my thoughts to sludge, my body to a leaden shell. I'd stare at the small, barred window in my room, watching rain streak the glass or birds soar beyond my reach, and wonder if I'd ever feel whole again.

The diagnosis came like a thunderclap: paranoia. It stung, a cruel mislabeling of my reality. I wasn't paranoid—I was a new mother, navigating the overwhelming tide of emotions that crash over you after childbirth. The exhaustion that seeps into your bones, the hormonal shifts that leave you raw, the quiet terror of not being enough—these were the baby blues, a rite of passage for so many women, yet one we're taught to hide. I wasn't delusional; I was human. But instead of a hand to lift me up, I got a label to pin me down. They dismissed my tears as madness, my pleas as instability, stripping away my identity as a mother and leaving me to question my own mind. Was I losing myself? For a fleeting moment, I doubted. But beneath the fog, I knew the truth: I was being wronged, betrayed by a system too quick to judge and too slow to listen.

Yet amidst the darkness, there was a flicker of light—my daughter. She survived, a tiny beacon of hope in a storm that threatened to drown me. I couldn't hold her as I longed to, couldn't soothe her cries or feel her warmth against my chest, but she was the thread that kept me tethered. One night, as I lay in that hospital bed, my limbs heavy from medication, a nurse—a rare soul with kindness in her eyes—sat beside me. She took my hand, her touch warm and steady, and whispered, "You're not alone. You're a mother, and your daughter needs you." Those words pierced the haze, reigniting a spark within me. I clung to them, to the image of my baby's face, and vowed to fight—not just for myself, but for her.

That fight forged a strength I didn't know I possessed, a resilience born from the ashes of pain and injustice. The suffering could have broken me, but I chose to let it shape me into something unbreakable. The road back was jagged, paved with moments of despair when the hospital's echoes haunted me— the clatter of trays, the murmur of distant voices, the weight of those drugs in my veins. But there were glimmers of hope too: a letter from a friend slipped under my door, a memory of my daughter's birth that refused to fade. Slowly, I pieced myself together, driven by the promise of the life we'd one day share.

As my daughter grew, I poured that strength into her. Now, at 11, she's a force—independent, wise beyond her years, and fiercely capable. I've taught her to stand alone when she must, to trust her instincts, to face the world with the resilience I learned through fire. I recall a morning when she was 7, dragging a chair to the kitchen counter with a determined grunt. She poured cereal into a bowl, splashing milk with a furrowed brow, and when some spilled, she didn't flinch. She grabbed a towel, wiped it up, and grinned at me. "I can do it, Mom," she said, her voice steady. That small act swelled my heart with pride, a testament to the spirit I'd nurtured in her.

More than independence, I've taught her acceptance—of me, of us, of the scars we carry. My mental health diagnosis, the labels they tried to define me by, the battles I've fought—they don't diminish me, and they don't touch the sanctity of our bond. I am her mother, a truth no system can erase. I've shown her that love doesn't demand perfection, that strength is rising through hardship, not avoiding it. We've built something extraordinary, a partnership tempered by adversity. We speak openly—about mental health, about asking for help, about the power of enduring. She knows it's okay to falter, that her value isn't tied to flawlessness. And in teaching her, I've forgiven myself for the days I felt I fell short.

She knows my story—how I clawed my way back for her, how the world tried to sever us but failed. She understands that mental health is a battle, not a weakness, one I've waged for her sake. In her eyes, I see healing—a reflection of the fire that kept me alive, now burning bright in her. There are still shadows, days when the past presses close, but her growth, her spirit, makes every struggle worthwhile. She's my triumph, my purpose, the living proof of a love that refused to break.

I am her mother—my truth, my identity, my north star. No hospital, no diagnosis, no lie can steal that from me. In her, I see the same unyielding flame that sustained me—a declaration: "I am here, I am strong, I will not be broken." In quiet moments, watching her sleep or lost in thought, I marvel at our journey. The nightmares have softened, overtaken by the glow of our shared resilience. Every trial has sculpted us into who we are, and I'm grateful for it.

This is my story, but it's hers too. Together, we've turned pain into power, an unbreakable duo ready for whatever lies ahead. I see a future vast with promise for her—a young woman unafraid to stand tall, to lift others as she rises. Her lessons, born from our path, will guide her, just as she inspires me. Our tale isn't merely survival; it's victory, a monument to a mother's love that no force could extinguish.

Chapter 5
EDUCATION

After the tumultuous experiences of my earlier years and the profound journey of motherhood, I found myself at a crossroads. I had survived so much—misunderstandings, labels, and the heart-wrenching loss of my children to the system. Yet, through it all, a spark of determination remained within me. I wanted more for myself and for my daughter, whom I had fought so hard to keep in my life. I wanted to prove, not just to the world but to myself, that I was capable of achieving something significant despite the shadow of schizophrenia that loomed over me. That's when I decided to pursue a Bachelor's degree in Health and Social Care, driven by a desire to understand and improve the systems that had so profoundly impacted my life.

Choosing to go back to school was not an easy decision. The thought of stepping into a classroom again filled me with both excitement and dread. Excitement because education represented a path to a better future, a way to gain knowledge and skills that could open doors and perhaps allow me to help others like me. Dread because I feared the judgment and misunderstanding that had followed me throughout my life—from my childhood in a fractured family, through the misdiagnoses in psychiatric wards, to the dismissive attitudes of my own kin. Would my mental health diagnosis become a barrier once more? Would people see me as less capable because of it?

Despite these fears, I enrolled in a local college, determined to earn my Bachelor's degree. From the very beginning, the journey was fraught with obstacles. Financially, it was a struggle. I had to juggle part-time jobs—cleaning offices late at night or serving tables when my energy allowed—to pay for tuition and living expenses, all while managing my mental health and being a mother to my daughter. There were days when the weight of it all felt unbearable, when the symptoms of my illness flared up—paranoia whispering doubts in my ears or exhaustion pinning me to my bed—making it hard to concentrate or even show up to class. But I pushed through, clinging to the image of my daughter's proud smile and the goal I had set for us both.

One of the most significant challenges I faced was discrimination. It wasn't always overt, but it was there, lurking in the shadows like the stigma I'd carried for years. Some professors seemed to doubt my abilities, perhaps because they knew of my background through whispered rumors or sensed something different about me in my quieter moments. I remember one instance vividly: I approached a professor for help with an assignment, my hands trembling slightly from nerves. Instead of offering guidance, he looked at me with a pitying smile and suggested that maybe the course was too demanding for me, that I should consider something less challenging. His words stung, echoing the voices of my sisters who'd mocked me, the social workers who'd deemed me unfit, reinforcing the doubts I already had about myself.

Peers, too, could be unkind. Group projects were particularly difficult. I often felt excluded or dismissed, as if my contributions weren't valuable. There was a sense that I didn't quite belong, that I was an outsider in this academic world—a feeling that harkened back to my childhood isolation and the holiday gatherings where I was sidelined. But amidst these challenges, I found support. I connected with a professor who saw potential in me beyond the labels and encouraged me to keep going. She became a mentor, offering both academic guidance and emotional support. Her belief in me was a beacon of hope during tough times.

After years of perseverance, I completed my Bachelor's degree in Health and Social Care. It was a moment of pride, but I knew my journey was not over. During my studies, I had become fascinated by psychology, particularly its insights into mental health—insights that resonated deeply with my own experiences with schizophrenia. This growing passion led me to pursue a Master's degree in Psychology, determined to deepen my understanding and contribute to the field.

Enrolling in the Master's program was both exhilarating and daunting. I was stepping into a new level of academia, where the expectations were higher, and the stakes felt greater. Yet, I was resolute. Studying psychology gave me insights into my own condition that were both humbling and empowering. Learning about schizophrenia—its symptoms, its treatments, its realities—helped demystify my experiences. It was as if I was meeting myself on the page, understanding that my struggles had a name, that they were not a personal failing but a medical condition that could be managed. This knowledge became a tool for self-acceptance. I began to recognize patterns in my thoughts and behaviors, developing coping mechanisms that made life more manageable—journaling to quiet the noise in my head, pacing my studies to avoid overwhelm. It also gave me the language to advocate for myself, to explain my needs to professors and peers when necessary, turning my vulnerability into a quiet strength.

However, the road was not without its setbacks. During my second year of the Master's program, the stress of exams, combined with the exhaustion of single motherhood and haunting memories of my lost children, triggered a relapse. Voices that I'd worked so hard to silence grew loud again, and I found myself questioning my reality. I had to take a leave of absence to focus on recovery, a decision that filled me with fear that I might never return to school. But with the support of my therapist, my mentor, and the thought of my daughter waiting for me at home, I did return, more determined than ever to complete my degree.

Finally, after years of hard work, sacrifices, and unwavering perseverance, the day of my graduation arrived. Standing there in my cap and gown, waiting to receive my Master's diploma in Psychology, I felt a surge of emotions—pride, relief, and a profound sense of accomplishment. My daughter sat in the audience, her grin wide and her cheers loud, a living testament to why I'd fought so hard. This degree was more than just a piece of paper; it was a symbol of everything I had overcome—the loneliness of my childhood, the losses of my twenties, the battles of motherhood, and the daily war with my own mind.

My educational journey did not end with my Master's degree. In the years that followed, I continued to advocate for mental health awareness and support for mothers facing similar challenges. My efforts were recognized when I was awarded an Honorary Doctorate in Social Care, a humbling acknowledgment of my contributions to the field. To equip myself with the skills to create sustainable change, I also completed a Mini Doctorate in Business Administration. Additionally, my curiosity led me to explore the intersections of theology and psychology, seeking to understand the spiritual dimensions of mental health and healing, which enriched my perspective both personally and professionally.

As I reflect on my journey, I see not just the degrees and accolades—my Bachelor's in Health and Social Care, my Master's in Psychology, my Honorary Doctorate in Social Care, my studies in theology and psychology, and my Mini Doctorate in Business Administration—but the growth, resilience, and hope that carried me through. Education gave me the tools to understand myself and the strength to redefine my life—not as a victim, but as a survivor, a mother, a scholar, and a woman unbroken.

Chapter 6
Spirituality

In the quiet moments when my mind roared louder than I could bear, or when the world turned its back, I found something steady—something bigger than me. It wasn't always a pew in a church or a prayer neatly folded into words. Sometimes it was the rustle of leaves on a Berkshire breeze, or the flicker of a candle I'd lit to chase away the dark. Spirituality became my lifeline, not a fix for the chaos of schizophrenia or the sting of rejection, but a soft place to land when everything else felt jagged. It's been my way of stitching meaning into a life that's often felt like a patchwork of pain and triumph.

It started young, back when I was a kid lost in a family that didn't feel like mine. I'd slip away to the woods near our house in Berkshire, where the trees didn't care that I was the odd one out. Under their branches, I'd breathe easier, feeling a peace I couldn't name. I didn't know it was spirituality then—just a kid's instinct to find comfort where I could. But those moments planted a seed, a quiet knowing that there was something out there, or maybe in me, that didn't judge or push me away.

When the misdiagnosis of paranoid schizophrenia hit me like a brick in my twenties, that seed started to grow into something I could hold onto. The psychiatric hospital was a cold, grey maze—meds that dulled me, staff who saw a label instead of a person. I felt stripped bare, my reality twisted by voices and doubts I couldn't always sort out. But in my little room, I'd close my eyes and picture those woods again, the earth solid under me. I started whispering prayers—not the stiff ones from childhood Sundays, but messy, honest ones. *"Give me strength. Help me make it through this. Keep my daughter safe."* It wasn't about erasing the illness; it was about finding the grit to face it. And somehow, it worked. I'd feel a calm settle in, like a hand on my shoulder saying, *"You're not alone."*

Family's always been a sore spot—those holiday tables where I was the scapegoat, the one who didn't fit. For years, I carried their rejection like a stone in my chest, wondering what I'd done to deserve it. Spirituality shifted that weight. Sitting in silence one Christmas after another snub, I let myself think it through. Maybe their coldness wasn't about me—maybe it was their own stuff, their own limits. I started praying for them, not out of some grand forgiveness, but to let go of the hurt for my own sake. It didn't fix everything—my sisters and I aren't suddenly best mates—but it gave me peace, a way to stop letting their words define me.

Motherhood, though—that's where spirituality really showed its muscle. When I was pregnant with my daughter, the system tried to rip her from me before she even took her first breath. They said I'd hurt her, that a "mad woman" couldn't be a mum. Every kick she gave me felt like a defiance of that lie, a little miracle saying, *"We're in this together."* I'd rest my hands on my belly and pray, fierce and quiet, for the strength to fight for her. After she was born, locked in that hospital with accusations flying, I'd whisper to whatever was listening—God, the universe, those Berkshire trees—begging for a way to keep her. And we made it. She's eleven now, bold and bright, and I know that connection to something greater carried us through. It wasn't just me fighting; it was us, plus that unseen force I leaned on.

Education was another battlefield where spirituality kept me standing. Going for my psychology degree, I faced late nights, tight money, and professors who looked at me like I was a lost cause. There were moments—exams looming, my mind foggy with paranoia—when I wanted to quit. One night, drowning in textbooks and doubt, I lit a candle and just sat with it. The flame danced, steady and sure, and I asked for clarity, for the will to keep going. I'd breathe slow, watching the light, and feel this quiet push—like a voice saying, *"You've got this."* Next morning, I'd crack those books again, fuelled by something deeper than caffeine. That degree's mine now, and I know it's not just hard work that got me there—it's that stubborn faith that wouldn't let me fall.

My spirituality's a bit of a mongrel, truth be told. It's not one religion with a rulebook—it's a mix of prayers when I'm desperate, meditation when I need calm, and walks where the wind feels like it's talking back. There've been times I've wondered if it's real, especially with schizophrenia muddying the waters. Is that peace I feel a gift, or just my mind playing tricks? But I've learned to trust it. The illness pulls me apart; spirituality pulls me together. That's the difference.

Not everyone gets it. Some see it as another sign I'm "off," like I'm chatting to imaginary friends. But my daughter—she sees it clear. She's grown up watching me light that candle or step outside to breathe under the sky, and she knows it's how I stay strong. I've taught her it's okay to lean on something bigger, that it's not weak to ask for help—whether from people or whatever's out there.

Now, spirituality's woven into who I am. It's changed as I have—deeper when I've needed it most, simpler when life's steadier. It's not about escaping the hard stuff; it's about facing it with something solid at my back. It's shown me I'm not just a diagnosis or a failure—I'm part of something vast, something that sees me even when I can't see myself. That's the real miracle, isn't it? Finding light in the dark, not because it fixes everything, but because it reminds you you're worth the fight.

Chapter 7
Overcoming Barriers

The road of my life has been no gentle path through a meadow—it's been a jagged trail carved through mountains, littered with boulders that seemed too heavy to move and cliffs that dared me to fall. Each step has been a battle against barriers that loomed like storm clouds, threatening to drown me in doubt, stigma, and despair. Yet, here I stand, weathered but unbroken, my heart still beating with the rhythm of resilience. The story of how I overcame these barriers isn't one of effortless triumphs or fairy-tale endings. It's raw, messy, and real—a tapestry woven from tears, grit, and the stubborn refusal to let the world define me.

The first barrier I faced was the weight of misunderstanding, a shadow that clung to me from childhood. Growing up in a family where I felt like an outsider, I learned early that my voice could be dismissed, my presence overlooked. My sisters' sharp words and my parents' stormy battles built a wall between me and belonging, brick by brick. At school, the cruelty of classmates only added more stones, each taunt a reminder that I didn't fit. This wasn't just rejection—it was a message, seeping into my bones, whispering that I was less than, unworthy of love or respect. That message could have crushed me, and for a time, it nearly did. I retreated into myself, my self-esteem crumbling like dry leaves underfoot. But somewhere deep inside, a spark flickered—a quiet defiance that refused to let their judgment be my truth.

That spark grew into a flame when I faced the next barrier: the misdiagnosis of paranoid schizophrenia. In my twenties, when the world should have been opening up, it slammed shut instead. The psychiatric hospital, with its sterile corridors and heavy medications, wasn't a place of healing—it was a cage where I was stripped of agency and branded "mad." The label of schizophrenia wasn't just a medical term; it was a scarlet letter, branding me as unreliable, dangerous, unfit. It followed me into every corner of my life—relationships frayed, opportunities vanished, and even my own mind turned traitor, whispering doubts I couldn't always silence. The stigma was suffocating, a barrier not just to my freedom but to my sense of self. How do you fight a world that's already decided who you are?

I fought by clawing my way back to clarity, inch by painful inch. Therapy became my map, helping me navigate the tangled roots of my pain. Medication, when adjusted properly, quieted the storm enough for me to think. But the real weapon was my own stubborn will. I refused to let that label define me. I journaled relentlessly, spilling my fears onto pages that didn't judge. I sought out stories of others who'd been misdiagnosed or misunderstood, finding solace in their survival. And I leaned on spirituality—those whispered prayers to the Berkshire trees, to God, to the universe—begging for the strength to keep going. Each small step forward was a victory, a crack in the barrier that said I could be more than my diagnosis.

Motherhood brought the steepest barrier of all: a system that deemed me unfit to love my own children. When my daughter was born, the joy of her first cry was drowned out by accusations—claims that I'd harm her, that a woman with my history couldn't be trusted. The pain of those words was a blade, cutting deeper than any loss I'd known. Losing my earlier children to adoption had already left scars, but this—this was a fresh wound, raw and bleeding. The social workers, with their clipboards and cold efficiency, didn't see a mother fighting for her baby; they saw a case file, a risk to be managed. The psychiatric hospital became my prison again, its walls echoing with the lie that I was a danger to the one person I'd die to protect.

Overcoming that barrier took every ounce of my being. I fought with love—fierce, unyielding love for my daughter. Every night in that hospital, I'd close my eyes and picture her tiny face, her kicks from when she was still inside me, and I'd vow to prove them wrong. A kind nurse, a rare ally, slipped me hope with her words: "You're a mother, and your daughter needs you." I clung to that truth like a lifeline. I complied with the system's demands—swallowed the pills, attended the sessions—not because I believed their narrative, but because I knew it was the only way to get back to her. And when I finally held her again, her warmth against my chest, I knew no barrier could sever that bond. Love, I learned, is a force stronger than any institution, any label, any lie.

Education was another mountain, its slopes slick with discrimination and doubt. Enrolling in college for my Bachelor's in Health and Social Care was a leap of faith, a bet on myself when the odds felt stacked against me. The financial strain was relentless—late-night cleaning shifts, scraping together tuition, all while raising my daughter and managing my mental health. But the real barrier was the skepticism I faced. Professors who raised eyebrows at my questions, peers who sidelined me in group projects, their pity or disdain a silent echo of my childhood exclusion. One professor's suggestion that the course might be "too demanding" for me burned like acid, threatening to reignite old insecurities. It wasn't just about passing exams; it was about proving I belonged in a world that kept trying to push me out.

I overcame that barrier with dogged perseverance and a few unexpected allies. My mentor, a professor who saw my potential, became my north star, guiding me through the academic maze with encouragement and tough love. I learned to advocate for myself, explaining my needs when symptoms flared, refusing to let my diagnosis be an excuse for failure. My daughter's pride— her wide grin when I showed her my first A—fueled me through sleepless nights. And when I walked across that stage, cap and gown swaying, my Master's in Psychology in hand, I wasn't just a graduate. I was a warrior, having slain the doubts of others and my own.

The lessons I've learned from these barriers are etched into my soul, each one a hard-won gem. First, resilience isn't about never falling—it's about getting up, again and again, even when your knees are bloody. I fell plenty—relapses, rejections, moments when the voices in my head screamed louder than hope. But every time, I found a reason to rise: my daughter's laugh, a kind word from a friend, the flicker of a candle in the dark. Second, you can't wait for the world to understand you. I spent years craving acceptance from my family, from society, only to realize that my worth doesn't depend on their approval. I had to define myself—through my actions, my love, my fight.

Strategies? They're simple but not easy. I leaned on routine—small, grounding habits like morning walks or nightly journaling—to anchor me when my mind spun. I built a support network, not vast but solid: a therapist who listened, a mentor who believed, a friend who'd sit with me in silence. Spirituality was my compass, guiding me back to center when I wandered too far into doubt. And I learned to celebrate the small wins—a good day, a finished essay, a moment of clarity—because those are the stepping stones to bigger victories.

These barriers—misunderstanding, misdiagnosis, systemic judgment, discrimination—weren't just obstacles; they were forge fires, shaping me into someone stronger than I ever thought possible. They taught me that the world may set traps, but it can't steal your spirit unless you let it. I'm still climbing, still facing new cliffs, but I know now that no barrier is too big when you carry a flame inside you. That flame is my daughter, my faith, my story—a light that no darkness can extinguish.

Chapter 8
Embracing Success

As I look back on my life, I am struck by the journey I have travelled. It has been a path marked by pain, misunderstanding, and loss, but also by resilience, determination, and triumph. The challenges I have faced—being misdiagnosed with paranoid schizophrenia, struggling to be accepted by my family, fighting to keep my daughter, and battling discrimination in education—could have broken me. But instead, they have forged me into someone stronger, someone who has learned to embrace success not despite my struggles, but because of them.

When I decided to pursue a Bachelor's degree in Health and Social Care, it was a leap of faith. I had always loved learning, but my previous experiences with education had been tainted by the bullying and isolation I faced in school. The thought of stepping back into a classroom filled me with anxiety, but I knew that this was my chance to create a better future for myself and my daughter. I enrolled in a local college, determined to prove to myself and the world that I was more than my diagnosis.

From the very beginning, the journey was fraught with obstacles. Financially, it was a struggle. I had to juggle part-time jobs—cleaning offices late at night or serving tables when my energy allowed—to pay for tuition and living expenses, all while managing my mental health and being a mother to my daughter. There were days when the weight of it all felt unbearable, when the symptoms of my illness flared up—paranoia whispering doubts in my ears or exhaustion pinning me to my bed—making it hard to concentrate or even show up to class. But I pushed through, clinging to the image of my daughter's proud smile and the goal I had set for us both.

One of the most significant challenges I faced was discrimination. It wasn't always overt, but it was there, lurking in the shadows like the stigma I'd carried for years. Some professors seemed to doubt my abilities, perhaps because they knew of my background through whispered rumours or sensed something different about me in my quieter moments. I remember one instance vividly: I approached a professor for help with an assignment, my hands trembling slightly from nerves. Instead of offering guidance, he looked at me with a pitying smile and suggested that maybe the course was too demanding for me, that I should consider something less challenging. His words stung, echoing the voices of my sisters who'd mocked me, the social workers who'd deemed me unfit, reinforcing the doubts I already had about myself.

But amidst these challenges, I found support. I connected with a professor who saw potential in me beyond the labels and encouraged me to keep going. She became a mentor, offering both academic guidance and emotional support. Her belief in me was a beacon of hope during tough times. I also found solace in the library, where I could lose myself in books and research, discovering a passion for understanding the human mind and the systems that support—or fail—those in need.

As I progressed through my studies, I began to see the connections between my own experiences and the theories I was learning. Courses on mental health policy and social care ethics resonated deeply, giving me a framework to understand the injustices I had faced. I wrote papers on the stigma surrounding mental illness, drawing from my own life to illustrate the real-world impact of societal prejudices. My professors praised my insights, and for the first time, I felt that my voice mattered, that my experiences had value beyond my personal struggles.

After years of perseverance, I completed my Bachelor's degree in Health and Social Care. It was a moment of pride, but I knew my journey was not over. During my studies, I had become fascinated by psychology, particularly its insights into mental health—insights that resonated deeply with my own experiences with schizophrenia. This growing passion led me to pursue a Master's degree in Psychology, determined to deepen my understanding and contribute to the field.

Enrolling in the Master's programme was both exhilarating and daunting. I was stepping into a new level of academia, where the expectations were higher, and the stakes felt greater. Yet, I was resolute. Studying psychology gave me insights into my own condition that were both humbling and empowering. Learning about schizophrenia—its symptoms, its treatments, its realities—helped demystify my experiences. It was as if I was meeting myself on the page, understanding that my struggles had a name, that they were not a personal failing but a medical condition that could be managed. This knowledge became a tool for self-acceptance. I began to recognise patterns in my thoughts and behaviours, developing coping mechanisms that made life more manageable—journaling to quiet the noise in my head, pacing my studies to avoid overwhelm. It also gave me the language to advocate for myself, to explain my needs to professors and peers when necessary, turning my vulnerability into a quiet strength.

However, the road was not without its setbacks. During my second year of the Master's programme, the stress of exams, combined with the exhaustion of single motherhood and haunting memories of my lost children, triggered a relapse. Voices that I'd worked so hard to silence grew loud again, and I found myself questioning my reality. I had to take a leave of absence to focus on recovery, a decision that filled me with fear that I might never return to school. But with the support of my therapist, my mentor, and the thought of my daughter waiting for me at home, I did return, more determined than ever to complete my degree.

Finally, after years of hard work, sacrifices, and unwavering perseverance, the day of my graduation arrived. Standing there in my cap and gown, waiting to receive my Master's diploma in Psychology, I felt a surge of emotions—pride, relief, and a profound sense of accomplishment. My daughter sat in the audience, her grin wide and her cheers loud, a living testament to why I'd fought so hard. This degree was more than just a piece of paper; it was a symbol of everything I had overcome—the loneliness of my childhood, the losses of my twenties, the battles of motherhood, and the daily war with my own mind.

My educational journey did not end with my Master's degree. In the years that followed, I continued to advocate for mental health awareness and support for mothers facing similar challenges. My efforts were recognised when I was awarded an Honorary Doctorate in Social Care, a humbling acknowledgment of my contributions to the field. To equip myself with the skills to create sustainable change, I also completed a Mini Doctorate in Business Administration. Additionally, my curiosity led me to explore the intersections of theology and psychology, seeking to understand the spiritual dimensions of mental health and healing, which enriched my perspective both personally and professionally.

As I reflect on my journey, I see not just the degrees and accolades—my Bachelor's in Health and Social Care, my Master's in Psychology, my Honorary Doctorate in Social Care, my studies in theology and psychology, and my Mini Doctorate in Business Administration—but the growth, resilience, and hope that carried me through. Education gave me the tools to understand myself and the strength to redefine my life—not as a victim, but as a survivor, a mother, a scholar, and a woman unbroken.

Motherhood has been another source of profound success in my life. When my daughter was born, the system tried to take her from me, deeming me a danger because of my mental health. But I fought with every ounce of my being to keep her, and today, she is a testament to that love and determination. Now eleven years old, she is independent, wise beyond her years, and fiercely capable. I have taught her to stand tall, to trust her instincts, and to face the world with resilience. Watching her grow into the remarkable young woman she is becoming fills me with a pride that words cannot fully capture.

One memory stands out: when she was seven, she dragged a chair to the kitchen counter, determined to pour her own cereal. She spilled some milk, but instead of getting upset, she grabbed a towel, cleaned it up, and grinned at me. "I can do it, Mum," she said, her voice steady. In that moment, I saw the strength and independence I had nurtured in her, and I knew that despite everything, I had succeeded as a mother.

But my journey as a mother has not been without its challenges. Raising a child while managing schizophrenia is a delicate balance. There are days when the symptoms flare up, and I worry about how it might affect her. I remember one evening when I was struggling with paranoia, convinced that someone was watching us through the windows. My daughter, sensing my distress, came over and took my hand. "It's okay, Mum," she said softly. "We're safe." Her calm reassurance grounded me, reminding me that I was not alone in this fight.

I have always been open with her about my condition, explaining it in age-appropriate ways as she grew older. I wanted her to understand that mental illness is not something to be ashamed of, but rather a part of who I am—a part that I manage with medication, therapy, and self-care. She has learned to recognise when I need space or when I need her support, and in turn, I have learned to lean on her in ways that are healthy and empowering for both of us.

Our relationship is built on mutual respect and understanding. I have taught her the importance of empathy, not just for me, but for others who may be struggling. She has a natural compassion for people, often volunteering at local shelters or organising fundraisers for mental health charities. I am proud to say that she has inherited my fighting spirit and my desire to make the world a better place.

As she enters her teenage years, I know that new challenges await us. But I am confident that the foundation we have built together will carry us through. She is my greatest success, my reason for fighting, and my source of endless joy.

Beyond my personal achievements, I have found success in advocating for others. My experiences with the mental health system and the challenges of motherhood have driven me to raise awareness and support those who feel voiceless. I have spoken at conferences, sharing my story with audiences of healthcare professionals, policymakers, and fellow survivors. I have written articles for mental health journals and blogs, offering insights into the realities of living with schizophrenia and the importance of compassionate care.

One of my most rewarding experiences was starting a support group for mothers with mental health challenges. I remember the first meeting, held in a small community centre. Only a handful of women showed up, but as we shared our stories, I could see the relief in their eyes—the realisation that they were not alone. Over time, the group grew, and we became a tight-knit community, offering each other support, resources, and hope.

My advocacy work has also led me to collaborate with organisations dedicated to reforming the mental health system. I have lobbied for better training for social workers and healthcare providers, emphasising the need for empathy and understanding when working with individuals like me. My efforts have not gone unnoticed, and I was honoured to receive an Honorary Doctorate in Social Care for my contributions to the field.

But perhaps the most meaningful recognition comes from the people I have helped along the way. I receive letters and emails from individuals who have read my story or attended my talks, thanking me for giving them hope and inspiring them to keep fighting. These messages are a reminder that my struggles have not been in vain—they have given me a platform to make a difference in the lives of others.

As I reflect on my journey, I am filled with a sense of gratitude for the lessons I have learned and the person

I have become. Each achievement—whether it be my degrees, my role as a mother, or my advocacy work—has been a step toward healing. They have allowed me to reclaim the parts of myself that were once lost to pain and doubt, and to redefine my identity on my own terms.

I have learned that success is not about perfection, but about persistence. It is about showing up, even when the odds are against you, and believing that you are worthy of the dreams you chase. My journey has taught me that resilience is not a fixed trait, but a muscle that grows stronger with each challenge faced. And while the road has been difficult, it has also been filled with moments of joy, love, and connection.

To anyone reading this who feels weighed down by their own struggles, I want to say this: your story is not defined by the barriers you face but by the strength you show in overcoming them. Success is not a distant dream reserved for others—it is within your reach, no matter how impossible it may seem. My journey is proof that even in the darkest moments, there is light to be found. Embrace your resilience, hold onto your determination, and know that you, too, can turn your pain into power.

As I stand here today, I am not just a survivor of adversity—I am a testament to the miracles that can happen when you refuse to give up. My successes are not the end of my story but a new beginning, a reminder that no matter what life throws at you, you have the strength to rise.

Chapter 9:
A New Chapter: Living with Purpose

Looking back on my journey, I am amazed at the strength I didn't know I had. The pain and struggles were real—being misunderstood by my family, misdiagnosed with paranoid schizophrenia, and fighting to keep my daughter—but so were the victories. Each challenge taught me something valuable, and I carry those lessons with me every day. What once felt like insurmountable barriers—my fractured childhood, the weight of stigma, the loss of my earlier children, and the battle for motherhood—have become the foundation of my resilience. I am no longer defined by the labels others placed on me. Instead, I define myself by the life I have built, the love I have nurtured, and the purpose I have found.

Today, I live in a cozy one-bedroom flat in London with my daughter, now a bright and independent eleven-year-old. Our home is alive with the cheerful chatter of our birds—two doves, two Australian parrots, and four lovebirds—whose songs remind me daily of the beauty in life's small moments. My mornings begin with meditation and a slow walk, practices that ground me and prepare me for the day ahead. These rituals, rooted in my spiritual journey, help me manage the ongoing challenges of living with schizophrenia. Some days are harder than others—there are still moments when the voices creep in or paranoia clouds my thoughts—but I have learned to navigate them with grace. Therapy, medication, and the unwavering support of my daughter keep me steady. I am not trapped by my diagnosis; I live with it, but it does not own me.

My experiences have ignited a passion for helping others, and advocacy has become a cornerstone of my life. I now work with organizations that support mothers facing mental health challenges, offering the guidance and understanding I once desperately needed. Through speaking engagements, writing, and community outreach, I share my story to inspire hope and drive change. Recently, I spoke at a conference for mental health professionals, emphasizing the importance of empathy in care. After my talk, a young woman approached me, tears in her eyes, and said, "Your story gives me hope that I can overcome my struggles too." Moments like these remind me why I do this work. They fuel my mission to ensure that no one else feels as alone as I once did.

Motherhood remains my greatest source of joy and pride. My daughter is now a teenager, and our bond is stronger than ever. She has grown into a compassionate and resilient young woman, wise beyond her years. I see in her the strength I fought so hard to nurture. We support each other in ways that are both tender and powerful—she knows my struggles, and I know her dreams. Together, we have built a relationship rooted in trust, love, and mutual respect. I have always been open with her about my mental health, and she has learned to approach it with empathy and understanding. When I have difficult days, she is there with a quiet reassurance: "It's okay, Mum. We're safe." Her presence is a constant reminder that love can heal even the deepest wounds.

Education continues to be a lifeline for me. I am always seeking new ways to understand myself and the world around me. Recently, I have been exploring the intersection of mental health and spirituality, finding insights that enrich both my personal and professional life. I am also pursuing further studies in psychology, eager to deepen my knowledge and contribute to the field that has given me so much. Learning is not just a pursuit; it is a way to keep growing, to keep evolving.

As I reflect on my journey, I am filled with gratitude for the miracles that have unfolded along the way. The pain of my past has not disappeared, but it has transformed into something meaningful—a source of strength, wisdom, and purpose. To anyone reading this who feels lost or defined by their struggles, know that you are not alone. Your journey is unique, but the strength to overcome is within you. Embrace your resilience, seek support, and never stop believing in your ability to create a life of purpose and joy. Success is not a distant dream reserved for others—it is within your reach, no matter how impossible it may seem.

As I stand here today, I look forward to the adventures that lie ahead, knowing that whatever comes my way, I have the tools and the heart to face it. My story is not over; it is just beginning a new chapter. And in this chapter, I live with purpose, guided by the lessons of my past and the hope for a future where every struggle is met with strength, every setback with grace, and every victory with gratitude.

Chapter 10:
Epilogue

As I sit here, penning the final pages of this memoir, I am filled with a sense of awe at the journey I have traveled. Life has not been easy—there were times when the weight of my struggles felt too heavy to bear, when the darkness seemed endless. But through it all, I have learned that even in the bleakest moments, there is light to be found. My story is one of immense challenges, but it is also one of immense miracles—miracles of strength, love, and the unyielding human spirit.

Looking back, I see a young girl who felt lost in a world that didn't understand her. I was misunderstood by my family, labeled by a system that failed to see my true self, and faced with the heartbreak of losing my children. The misdiagnosis of paranoid schizophrenia, the stigma that followed, and the battles I fought to keep my youngest daughter could have defined me. But I refused to let them. Instead, I chose to define myself by the strength I found within, by the love I have for my daughters, and by the purpose I discovered in helping others.

Education became my lifeline. It was through my studies—my degree in Health and Social Care, my 20 diplomas, my mini doctorate in Business Administration—that I began to understand the systems that had once oppressed me. Knowledge gave me power, not just to change my own life, but to advocate for others who feel voiceless. My advocacy work, recognized with an Honorary Doctorate in Social Care, has become a way to turn my pain into purpose. Every time I speak at a conference, lead a support group, or write an article, I am reminded that my story has the power to inspire hope in others. And that, to me, is the greatest success of all.

Motherhood, too, has been a source of profound joy and growth. My three daughters are my heart, each one a testament to the love that has carried me through the darkest times. Though the loss of my earlier children still aches, my youngest daughter, now eleven, is a daily reminder of what I have fought for. She is independent, compassionate, and wise beyond her years, and our bond is unbreakable. Together, we have built a life filled with laughter, love, and the cheerful songs of our pets—two doves, two Australian parrots, and four lovebirds—who fill our one-bedroom flat with life.

My relationships with my mum and sister have also healed over time. Where there was once distance and misunderstanding, there is now friendship and support. It is a testament to the power of forgiveness and the possibility of growth, even in the most fractured of families.

Spirituality has been my anchor through it all. In the quiet moments of meditation or the peace of a slow walk, I find clarity and strength. It has taught me to accept myself, to embrace my journey, and to find meaning in the struggles I have faced. Living with schizophrenia is not something that goes away—it is a part of me, but it does not define me. I have learned to manage it with grace, with the help of therapy, medication, and the love of those around me. Each day is a new opportunity to grow, to learn, and to live with purpose.

As I close this chapter of my life, I want to leave you with a message of hope. If there is one thing I have learned, it is that no matter how dark the road may seem, there is always a way forward. Your struggles do not define you—they are simply part of your story. What defines you is your resilience, your ability to rise after every fall, and your refusal to give up on yourself.

To anyone who feels weighed down by their own challenges, know this: you are stronger than you realize. Seek support, embrace your unique journey, and never stop believing in the possibility of a life filled with joy and purpose. My story is proof that even in the face of immense adversity, miracles are possible. You, too, can turn your pain into power, your struggles into strength, and your dreams into reality.

As I look to the future, I am filled with gratitude for the lessons I have learned and the person I have become. My journey is far from over—there are still mountains to climb and dreams to chase—but I face them with a heart full of hope and a spirit that refuses to be broken. This is not the end; it is simply a new beginning. And in this new chapter, I will continue to live with purpose, guided by the immense miracles that have brought me here.

www.ingramcontent.com/pod-product-compliance
Lightning Source LLC
Chambersburg PA
CBHW061732070526
44583CB00024B/3102